I·N·S·I·D·E
THE
NETHERLANDS

Ian James

Franklin Watts
London · New York · Sydney · Toronto

CONTENTS

© 1990 Franklin Watts
96 Leonard Street
London EC2A 4RH

Published in the USA by
Franklin Watts Inc.
387 Park Avenue South
New York, N.Y. 10016

Franklin Watts Australia
14 Mars Road
Lane Cove
NSW 2066

Design: K & Co
Illustrations: Hayward Art Group

UK ISBN: 0 7496 0113 2
US ISBN: 0-631-14044-X
Library of Congress Catalog
Card Number: 89-49504

Phototypeset by Lineage Ltd, Watford
Printed in Belgium
All rights reserved

Photographs: David Simson of
Das Photo

Additional Photographs:
The Bridgeman Art Library/National
Gallery 21; The J Allen Cash
Photolibrary 15; Courtauld Institute
Galleries, London (Courtauld
Galleries) 22; CFCL/Dorothy Burrows
10, 11B; CFCL/Chris Fairclough 30;
National Maritime Museum, London 7;
thanks to the Netherlands Board of
Tourism 6, 18T; Popperfoto 8T, 8B;
Betty Rawlings 16B, 25, 26; Frank
Spooner Pictures, J Paireault 28.

Front cover: Zefa
Back cover: Zefa
Frontispiece: David Simson

The land

The Netherlands is a small but densely populated country in Western Europe. It is one of the Low Countries, so called because most of the land is low-lying. More than two-fifths of the country was once under water. But the Dutch have dug canals and built sea walls, called dykes, to hold back the sea.

Areas reclaimed from the sea are called polders. They are below sea level at high tide, and make up more than a quarter of the country. The Netherlands has suffered several major floods, when high storm waves have burst through the sea walls. But the Dutch then built even stronger walls. The people have a saying: "God created the Earth, but the Dutch created the Netherlands."

Below: **Dunes and dykes (sea walls) border much of the North Sea coast of the Netherlands.**

Above: **Canals criss-cross much of the country. Banks are built up along the canals to stop the water overflowing.**

Right: **The sandy plains in the east are mostly infertile. Pine forests and heathland cover large areas.**

Sand dunes border most of the coast. Inland, beyond the flat and generally fertile polders, are low, sandy hills, where pine forests grow. The country's highest point, 321 m (1,053ft) above sea level, is located in the far south. The Maas (or Meuse) river and the Lek and Waal, branches of the Rhine, flow across the south-central part of the country. The Schelde River enters the Netherlands from Belgium in the southwest.

The Netherlands has a mild climate. The rainfall averages 69 to 86 cm (27-34 inches) a year. Some rain occurs in every month.

Above: **During cold spells in winter, people enjoy skating on frozen lakes and canals.**

The people and their history

The Netherlands has been a mainly independent country since the late 16th century. It became a great world naval power in the 17th century. Its navigators were the first Europeans to explore the southwest Pacific. The Dutch built up a large empire, which included Indonesia. The Netherlands Antilles in the Caribbean Sea, is a fragment of that empire.

Wars with England and France in the 17th and 18th centuries weakened the Netherlands. England became the world's leading naval power and, in 1795, France invaded the Netherlands. Britain took many Dutch overseas possessions.

The Dutch drove out the French in 1813, and, in 1815, the Netherlands, Belgium and Luxembourg formed an independent kingdom. Belgium broke away in 1830 and Luxembourg in 1890.

Below: **The English and Dutch were rival naval powers in the 17th and 18th centuries. The picture shows the Battle of Texel in 1653, the final battle in the first Anglo-Dutch War.**

Left: **World War II caused great destruction in the Netherlands. Arnhem was the scene of a battle in 1944 between German soldiers and British and Polish paratroops.**

Below: **Storm waves smashed sea walls in January 1953, flooding more than 4 percent of the Netherlands. A new system of sea walls now protects the southwestern delta region.**

German troops invaded the country on May 10, 1940, and Japan occupied the Dutch East Indies (now Indonesia) in 1942. The war caused much destruction. Afterwards the Dutch set about rebuilding their country. They gradually gave their overseas possessions independence.

The Netherlands, Belgium and Luxembourg set up an economic union, called Benelux, in 1948. These three countries became founding members of the European Community in 1957.

Since 1957, the Netherlands has become a prosperous country. It is a constitutional monarchy, with an elected parliament headed by a prime minister and cabinet.

Above: **Queen Beatrix is the Head of State in the Netherlands. She became queen in 1980 when her mother, Queen Juliana, retired.**

Towns and cities

In 1987, only 12 percent of the Dutch people lived in the countryside. The rest lived in cities and towns.

Rotterdam, one of the world's busiest ports, serves not only the Netherlands, but also, via one of the branches of the Rhine River, parts of West Germany, France and Switzerland. Rotterdam developed quickly after the completion of the deep Nieuw Waterweg (New Waterway) in 1872, linking it to the North Sea. Its huge new port and industrial area, Europoort, stands on the Nieuw Waterweg on the coast. The Hague ('s-Gravenhage) is the Dutch seat of government. It contains the Queen's official residence and the International Court of Justice.

Above: **The Netherlands contains many attractive villages and small towns, which often stand on canals.**

Left: **Central Rotterdam is about 30 Km (19 miles) from the North Sea.**

Below: **The Royal Palace in The Hague ('s-Gravenhage) is the official residence of the Queen of the Netherlands.**

Left: **The historic city of Utrecht has many old churches. The tower in the photograph is all that remains of the Dom Cathedral which was destroyed by a hurricane in 1674.**

Utrecht, the fourth largest city in the Netherlands, contains many old buildings, including the house of Adrian VI, the only Dutch pope.

Groningen, the largest city in the north, also has many old buildings, including a university founded 1614. By contrast, Eindhoven and Tilburg are important industrial cities. Eindhoven is famous for its electrical and electronics factories.

Below: **The map shows major routes and cities in the Netherlands.**

Amsterdam, the country's capital and chief commercial and cultural city, was founded in about 1200. It stood on the Zuider Zee (now IJsselmeer), but much of this sea inlet has been drained to create polders. Canals now link Amsterdam to the sea. and it is the

Beautiful houses line Amsterdam's many canals. Tourist attractions include the Rijksmuseum, a major art gallery, the Van Gogh Museum, with many works by Vincent van Gogh, and Rembrandt House, former home of the painter Rembrandt van Rijn. Many people also visit the Anne Frank house, where Anne and her family hid during the German occupation of the Netherlands in World War II.

Above: **The Rijksmuseum in Amsterdam contains a magnificent collection of Dutch painting.**

Family life

The Netherlands is one of the most prosperous countries in Europe and its hard-working people enjoy a high standard of living. The average life expectancy at birth is 77 years. The country has an elaborate social welfare system. Most people get government benefits, including free medical treatment, and pensions for the elderly, widows and orphans.

Most people have attractive, comfortable and tidy homes, often with large windows that let in as much sunlight as possible. The Dutch spend a lot of time at home. They consider family life to be important and they hold celebrations on such occasions as birthdays, anniversaries and festivals. Most families enjoy outdoor activities.

Below: **The Netherlands has many peaceful villages, but in recent years more and more families have moved into the cities and towns.**

Above: **Large windows to let in sunlight are common features in homes in the Netherlands.**

Left: **Rows of elegant and beautifully preserved houses line the canals of Amsterdam.**

Food

Breakfast in the Netherlands usually consists of bread, spiced cake, sliced meat, cheese, jam and sometimes a boiled egg, with tea or coffee. Some popular lunch dishes include pancakes, salads and *uitsmijters,* consisting of bread and butter, with ham or cheese, and two fried eggs. Raw herrings and smoked eels are often sold from street stalls. The evening meal often consists of a soup, meat with fresh vegetables, followed by fruit or yogurt.

Asian food, including the Indonesian *Rijsttafel,* which consists of many spicy dishes served with rice, is popular. The cities and towns also have many Chinese and French restaurants.

Below: **This street market is in Delft, a town known for its magnificent pottery.**

Right: **Indonesian food is popular in the Netherlands. It is a reminder of the time when Indonesia was a Dutch colony.**

Below: **An open-air restaurant in Leiden, the birthplace of the painter Rembrandt van Rijn.**

Sports and pastimes

Soccer, hockey and basketball are leading team sports. In winter, ice skating is popular when the temperatures are low enough. In the Eleven Towns Race, ice skaters follow a 200-km (124-mile) course, linking 11 towns, along the frozen canals in the northern province of Friesland.

Popular festivals include St. Nicholas' Eve on December 5, when the Dutch exchange gifts instead of on Christmas Day. At Easter, children hunt for painted eggs and eat Easter men, made from bread.

Spectacular flower festivals are held in spring in flower-growing regions. On April 30, the Queen's Birthday, many towns are decorated and parades are held.

Above: **Soccer is the leading team sport in the Netherlands.**

Above: **St. Nicholas (Santa Claus) is the Dutch patron saint of children. St. Nicholas' Eve is a major festival celebrated with presents and parades.**

Left: **Bicycling is a popular activity. People often cycle to school or to work.**

The arts

The Netherlands is known for its beautiful glassware, tiles and Delft pottery. Its writers, apart from the scholar Desiderius Erasmus and the philosopher Baruch Spinoza, are little known outside the country. The most important literary figure was probably the 17th-century dramatist Joost van den Vondel. Dutch music is also little known outside the Netherlands, though most cities have concert halls and hold music festivals of all kinds. The Concertgebouw Orchestra of Amsterdam has an international reputation.

Painting is the art form for which the Netherlands is best known. Works by its great painters can be seen in galleries in all the major cities.

Below: *Belshazzar's Feast* **wa painted by Rembrandt van Rijn, the greatest painter of the Dutch Golden Age.**

Left: **A self-portrait by the Dutch painter, Vincent van Gogh.**

The 17th century, when the Netherlands was the world's leading naval power, was also the Golden Age of Dutch painting. Painters of this period included Frans Hals, Pieter de Hooch, Jacob van Ruisdael, Jan Vermeer, and, the greatest of all, Rembrandt van Rijn.

More recent artists include Vincent van Gogh, who lived in the second half of the 19th century, and Piet Mondrian, whose later work was based on geometrical patterns.

Farming

Farming employs only about five percent of Dutch workers, but it is extremely important. Farms cover about three-fifths of the land. Most farms are small, but farm yields are among the world's highest. The most important branch of farming is concerned with livestock. Most of the five million cattle are used to produce such dairy products as butter, cheese, and milk. Farmers also keep beef cattle, pigs, poultry and sheep.

Leading crops include barley, potatoes, sugar beet and wheat. Vegetables, flowers and bulbs, especially tulips, are also important. Fishing for herring, mackerel and flatfish is carried on in the North Sea and the country also has inshore fisheries.

Below: **Dutch farmers use machinery and fertilizers to get high yields from their land.**

Above: **About one-third of the Netherlands is devoted to grazing land.**

Left: **Fresh flowers and bulbs are grown in the western Netherlands between Alkmaar and Leiden.**

Industry

The Netherlands is one of the world's leading producers of natural gas. It also produces some petroleum. However, it lacks most of the raw materials needed by industry and these materials are imported. Because the land is so flat, hydro-electricity is unimportant and most of the electricity supply comes from power stations burning coal, oil or gas, with 6 percent from nuclear power stations.

Industry employs 32 percent of the workforce, as compared with 63 percent in services. The industrial workers are highly skilled and the Netherlands is a major industrial power. It is also one of the world's top trading nations. Shipping, banking and other financial services are also important.

Below: **Delft is known for its pottery, including so-called peacock pottery.**

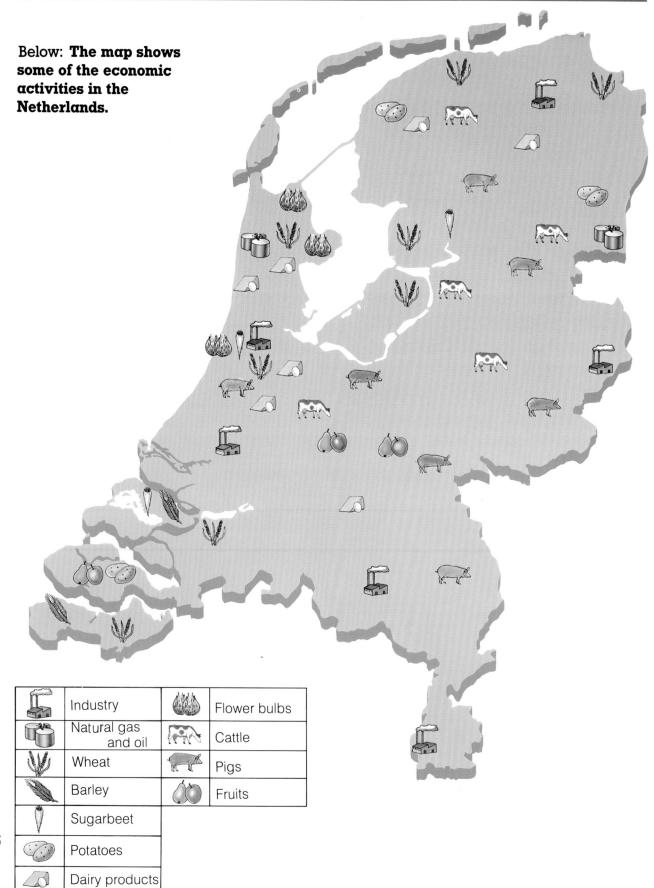

Below: **The map shows some of the economic activities in the Netherlands.**

	Industry		Flower bulbs
	Natural gas and oil		Cattle
	Wheat		Pigs
	Barley		Fruits
	Sugarbeet		
	Potatoes		
	Dairy products		

26

The country has some traditional industries, including diamond cutting in Amsterdam and porcelain making. Major products of the food-processing industries include butter, cheese, chocolate, eggs, cooked meats and milk. Oil and other raw materials imported through Rotterdam are used to make a wide range of chemical and petroleum products. Eindhoven is the headquarters of Philips, one of the world's leading electrical and electronics firms. Factories in Eindhoven make radios, television sets, and many other household appliances. The Netherlands also produces cars, machinery, ships, steel, textiles and many other items.

Below: **Europoort is a new port and industrial area on the western side of Rotterdam.**

Looking to the future

Throughout history, the Dutch have faced many challenges and they take great pride in their achievements in emerging triumphantly from many disasters. Since 1945, the country has rebuilt its cities and industries that had suffered great destruction in World War II. The Dutch responded in a similar way to the disastrous floods in 1953. They launched the Delta Plan, which involved building huge dams across the mouth of the delta region in the southwest. Floodgates now control surges of high waves during severe storms.

In recent years, its economic success has owed much to its membership of the European Community.

Left: **Dutch engineers have built massive dams to hold back the sea. The latest project, the Delta Plan in the southwest, was opened in 1986.**

Economic success has caused pollution. It has resulted from the dumping of industrial wastes into rivers, the use of fertilizers on the land, emissions from power stations, and traffic fumes. Today, the control of pollution is a major political issue.

The Netherlands is especially endangered by the "greenhouse effect" which is caused by the increasing amount of carbon dioxide in the atmosphere. Because of the greenhouse effect, world temperatures are expected to rise. This will lead to the melting of ice around the poles and a rise in the sea level. This is an obvious threat to a low-lying country. It seems possible that the Netherlands will soon be facing a new chapter in its long battle against the sea.

Above: **Young people in the Netherlands are concerned about the protection of the environment in their small, crowded country.**

Facts about the Netherlands

Area:
40,844 sq km
(15,770 sq miles)

Population:
14,616,000

Capital:
Amsterdam

Largest cities:
Amsterdam (pop
692,000)
Rotterdam (574,000)
's-Gravenhage
  (The Hague,
444,000)
Utrecht (230,000)
Eindoven (191,000)
Groningen (168,000)
Tilburg (154,000)

Official language:
Dutch

Religion:
Christianity

Main exports:
Machinery and
transportation
equipment; food,
drink and tobacco;
chemicals and
chemical products;
mineral fuels; rubber
and synthetic
products; metals and
metal products

Unit of currency:
Guilder

The Netherlands compared with other countries

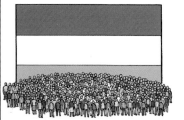

Netherlands 420 per sq km

UK 232 per sq km

USA 26 per sq km

Australia 2 per sq km

Above: **How many people?
The Netherlands is one of
the world's most densely
populated countries.**

Below: **How large? The
Netherlands is small. The
UK is nearly six times as
big as the Netherlands.**

UK

USA   Australia   Netherlands

Below: **Some money and stamps in the Netherlands.**

Index